EXILE ON A PEPPERCORN

MIRCEA DINESCU was born in the town of Slobozia, 120 kilometres east of Bucharest on 11th November 1950 and completed his secondary education in his native town. His first poem was published in 1967 by the journal *Luceafărul* for which he subsequently worked. More recently his poetry has been published in France, Italy, West Germany and the U.S.S.R. He is now on the editorial staff of *România Literară*.

☆ ☆ ☆

PETER FIELD (DIXIE) was born in Islington, London on 19th September 1950. He studied at Canterbury College of Art and was a professional musician until 1972. He now illustrates books and magazines, and writes satirical strips for publications such as *The New Statesman*, *The Listener*, *Punch*, and *Playboy*. He lectures internationally on cartoon and caricature, and his work appears on television as well as being frequently exhibited in major galleries in the United Kingdom.

EXILE ON A PEPPERCORN

THE POETRY OF
MIRCEA DINESCU

translated
by
ANDREA DELETANT
and
BRENDA WALKER
illustrations by
DIXIE
introduction by
DENNIS DELETANT

FOREST BOOKS
LONDON ☆ 1985 ☆ BOSTON

Published by FOREST BOOKS
20 Forest View, Chingford, London E4 7AY, U.K.
61 Lincoln Road, Wayland, M.A. 01788, U.S.A.

First published 1985

Typeset in Great Britain by Cover to Cover, Cambridge
Printed in Great Britain by A. Wheaton & Co. Ltd., Exeter

Jacket design and illustrations © Dixie
Poems © Mircea Dinescu
Translations © Andrea Deletant, Brenda Walker

All rights reserved

British Library Cataloguing in Publication Data
Dinescu, Mircea
Exile on a Peppercorn: the poetry of Mircea Dinescu.
I. Title   II. Deletant, Andrea   III. Walker, Brenda.
859'.134   PC840.19.D5
ISBN 0–948259–00–0

Library of Congress Catalog Card Number
85–080387

Acknowledgements

Poems have been taken from the following volumes:

Teroarea bunului simț/In Terror of Good Nature
(1980) Cartea Românească
A compendium based on the following:
Invocație nimănui (1971)
Elegii de cînd eram mai tînăr (1973)
Proprietarul de poduri (1976)
La dispoziția dumneavoastră (1979)

Democrația naturii/Nature's Democracy
(1981) Cartea Românească

Exil pe o boabă de piper/Exile on a Peppercorn
(1983) Cartea Românească

Contents

INTRODUCTION by Dennis Deletant   x

From   IN TERROR OF GOOD NATURE
          TEROAREA BUNULUI SIMŢ (1980)

The Cowardness of Writing Verse	3
(*Laşitatea de a scrie versuri*)	
At Your Disposal (*La dispoziţia dumneavoastră*)	5
In Terror of Good Nature (*Teroarea bunului simţ*)	6
Dynamite (*Dinamită*)	7
Lens (*Lentilă*)	8
The Bulldozer (*Buldozer*)	9
Chinese Nicknacks (*Chinezării*)	10
Parallel Lives (*Vieţi paralele*)	11
Snails' Chances (*Şansa melcilor*)	13
The Computer (*Computer*)	14
Transfiguration (*Schimbarea la faţă*)	15
Job in Love (*Iov îndrăgostit*)	16
Menagerie (*Bestiar*)	17
Letter to My Mother (*Scrisoare mamei*)	18
In all Innocence (*Candid*)	19
News in Brief (*Fapt divers*)	21
Refectory (*Cantina*)	22
A Couple (*Cuplu*)	23
Hired Sun (*Soare închiriat*)	24
The Contemporary Goat (*Capra contemporană*)	25
Rusting (*Ruginind*)	27
It's not Snowing (*Nu ninge*)	28
Absurd Chess (*Şah absurd*)	29
Evolution of Dream (*Evoluţia visului*)	30
Monologue with a Mouse (*Monolog cu un şoarece*)	31

From NATURE'S DEMOCRACY
DEMOCRAȚIA NATURII (1981)

Nature's Democracy (*Democrația naturii*)	35
Pest Control (*Deratizarea*)	37
Manuscript Found in a Bottle Lamp	38
(*Manuscris găsit într-o sticlă de lampă*)	
Some Advice for the Honeymoon	39
(*Cîteva sfaturi pentru luna de miere*)	
Travelling Players (*Teatru ambulant*)	41
Seven Drawers (*Șapte sertare*)	42
Skimpy Biography (*Biografie săracă*)	43
Walls (*Ziduri*)	45
Cold Comfort (*Indulgență de iarnă*)	46
Cows (*Vacile*)	47
Song (*Șansonetă*)	48
Avalanche (*Avalanșă*)	49
Love Story (*Love story*)	51
The Sign Searcher (*Căutătorul de semne*)	52
One Factory Calls for Another	53
(*O fabrică cheamă după ea o altă fabrică*)	
Discovering . . . (*Descoperirea operei*)	55
The Short-sighted Painter (*Pictorul miop*)	56
Speech Against Revolt (*Discurs împotriva revoltei*)	57
Village with Commuters (*Satul cu navetiști*)	58
A Short Extract from the Secret Files of the 100 Years War	59
(*Mic extras din dosarele secrete ale războiului de 100 de ani*)	
Hens (*Găinile*)	61
Titanic Waltz (*Titanic vals*)	62
The Fugitive (*Evadatul*)	63
How the Natives on the Reservation Lost the Right to Travel	65
(*Cum li s-a luat indigenilor din rezervație dreptul de a mai călători*)	
A Day Without Sandwiches (*O zi fără sandviș*)	67
With All Modesty (*Fără pretenții*)	68

* * *

Guernica (*Guernica*)	69
Hunger (*Foame*)	70

From **EXILE ON A PEPPERCORN**
EXIL PE O BOABĂ DE PIPER (1983)

Winter Diary at Pontus Euxinus (17 A.D.)	73
(*Jurnal de iarnă la Pontul Euxin*)	
Who are They Lord?! (*Cine sînt doamne?!*)	75
Postponed (*Se-amînă*)	76
Ship's Log (*Jurnal de bord*)	77
The Artist's Home (*Vila artistului*)	79
Song (*Cîntec de lampă stinsă*)	80
One of Armstrong's Tunes	81
(*O Melodie de Armstrong*)	
Exile on a Peppercorn (*Exile pe o boabă de piper*)	82

Any necessary changes in the text were made in consultation with Mircea Dinescu.

Introduction

Mircea Dinescu was only seventeen when the publication of his first poem caused a stir in literary circles. *Destin de familie* (Family Destiny) appeared in the journal *Luceafărul* on 9th September 1967. This same journal, then under the direction of Ştefan Bănulescu, continued to promote his work. His first collection *Invocaţie nimănui* (Invocation to No One) was published in 1971 and has been followed by *Elegii de cînd eram mai tînăr* (Elegies from My Younger Days) 1973, *Proprietarul de poduri* (The Owner of Bridges) 1976, *La dispoziţia dumneavoastră* (At Your Disposal) 1979, *Democraţia naturii* (Nature's Democracy) 1981, *Exil pe o boabă de piper* (Exile on a Peppercorn) 1983.

Dinescu is the angry young man of contemporary Romanian poetry, a moralist of the modern age. He admits to being born with anger:

Oh God how I was born
red with anger
crying out in an unknown tongue
    (Travelling Players)

and his own verse is conceived and delivered with violence:

> *For a long time I thought poetry slept beneath a heron's wing*
> *or that I'd have to forage for it in forests*
>
> *I'm now ready to make a pact with reality*
> *and admit to having been wrong:*
> *I'm smashing the wall with a pickaxe*
> *so you can see.*
>
> (Discovering . . .)

The poet's sense of revolt is directed at what we do to ourselves in the name of progress, and at what is done to us under the banner of utopianism. He vents his spleen at the manipulation of society, at

> *those who put concrete, glass and steel girders*
> *in the space from which God has fled.*
>
> (Exile on a Peppercorn)

What may have appeared in his early poems as a fit of rage has become in his later work almost an obsession characterized by its verbal aggressiveness. There is 'an anger within' him that 'feels like singing' (Menagerie), but the song is full of fury, ironic, infused sometimes with cynicism. His venom is the weapon of a ruthless judge, outraged at what has become of contemporary man. The contradictions of progress are underlined:

> *Stupid illusion*
> *to surround oneself with walls*
> *then suddenly to feel*
> *so free.*
>
> (Walls)

Even when the daily diet is 'tolerance and fear' (Cold Comfort), you are occasionally grateful that you have given up 'sandwiches for today'.

Dinescu's unexpected, novel and apparently random associations of words undermine our conceptions of the world about us and, fused with a mordant sarcasm, give an even keener cutting edge to his often epigrammatic observations:

A cold pair of scissors for cutting fingers
has nested in the letter box.

. . .

Death is freely available and cheap enough
while in contrast
there's great saving on fuel, paper and God.

If idiots were edible
there'd be a smaller queue at the butchers for intellectuals.

(Manuscript Found in a Bottle Lamp)

Unusual metaphors and similes bring his images into sharp focus:

As at a fair you pull out graves from a sleeve
dear Lord,
by the light of your dim halo
glory will polish its own boots

(Rusting)

A cap's a cloth shell
where I can lose my mind
like God in a balloon

(Song)

Dream-like sequences suggest a surrealist approach and yet irony directed at human behaviour brings his verse back to the realm of the conscious. Perverse semantic permutations should not, however, blind us to the warning that the poet gives of an incompatibility between traditional values and the patterns of life in contemporary society. Even the Christian faith is obsolete:

In the cars' cemetery I saw an angel rusting.

(Rusting)

Fantasy is used to express reality, the poet's imagery suggesting the tragic farce of the human condition:

In the evenings when orchestras turn to murder
and on waves of beer seven thousand drunkards leave for
America

(One of Armstrong's Tunes)

Somebody comes
with a deadly smelling cannister on his back:
'Who are they, those weak, wretched people
hidden behind the furniture?'

(Pest Control)

God Preserve me from those who want what's best for me
from the nice guys
always cheerfully ready to inform on me

(Cold Comfort)

At times this wretchedness is leavened by a measure of irony at the poet's own expense, reminiscent of his compatriot Marin Sorescu:

Get ready to love me
which means put on the white coat
buy me a wheelchair
take the laurel wreath from off my head
and with its leaves make me herbal tea instead

(Some Advice for the Honeymoon)

The poet offers no solution to the human predicament. Unlike Dostoievsky he does not believe that beauty will save the world but asserts that it is 'Sweet innocence to believe that poetry can improve the world' (Absurd Chess).

Dinescu's verse is strident and uncompromising; his wrath stems from a harrowed conscience, one which recognizes that the road to Utopia is paved with an intolerance that has degenerated into tyranny. There is an echo here of Osip Mandelstam's conclusion that 'there's no escaping the tyrant century'.

Dennis Deletant

from
In Terror of Good Nature
Teroarea bunului simț
(1980)

THE COWARDNESS OF WRITING VERSE

It's as if I were adjusting my song
to someone else's boredom
life jumps ahead of me:
builds a few restaurants on the shore
so I no longer know
if their music's trying to drown my cries
or accompany them
if revolt's the coward shade of action
the pub authentic
or the waves just a pretext

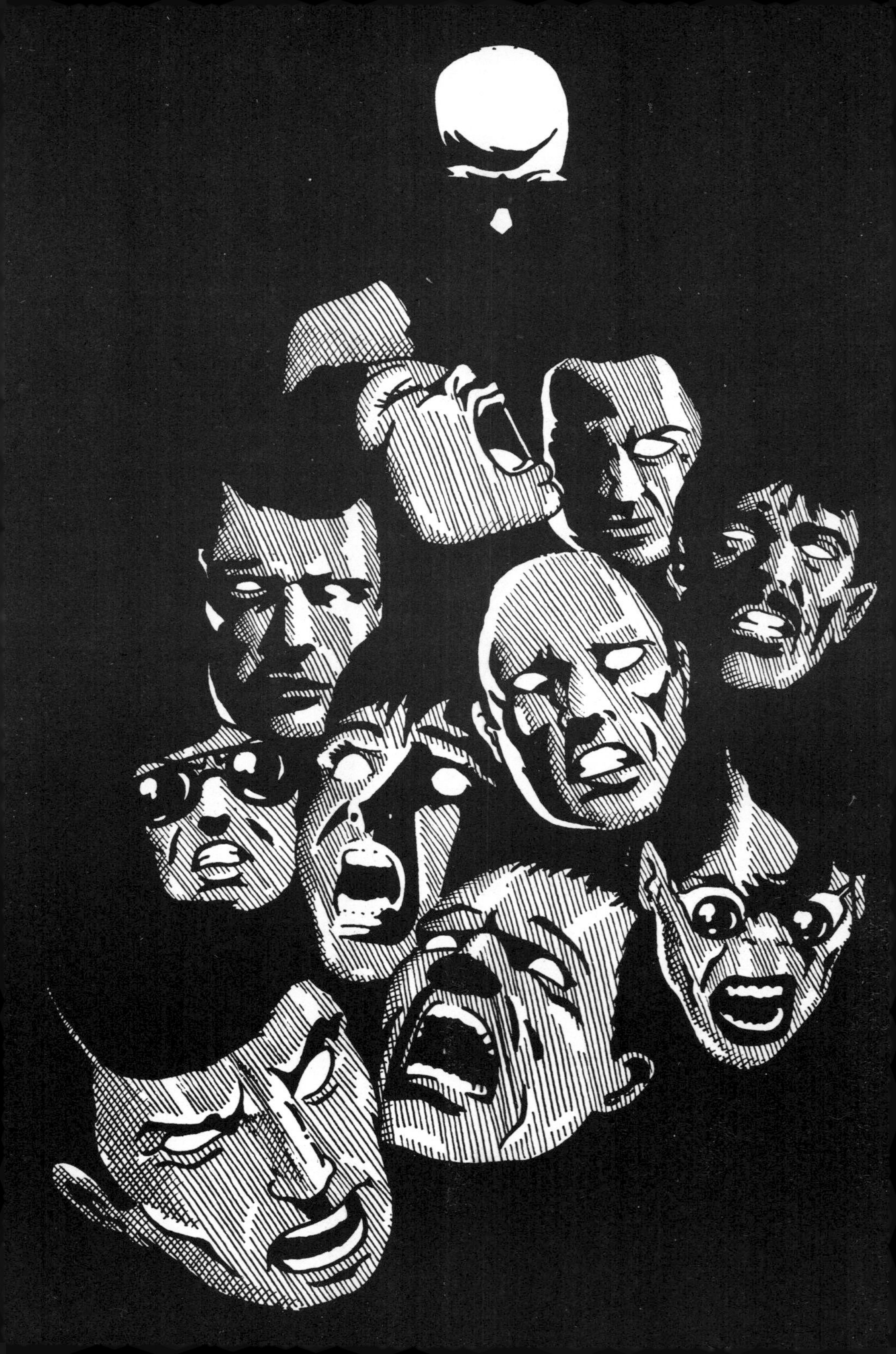

AT YOUR DISPOSAL

Misfortune travels through the neighbourhood in my orange shirt
and friends greet it absentmindedly
while I the milker of zeppelins drawn up into the air
between the wars,
answer them dangling pails above the furious crowd
which shouts and swears and points a finger:
'That man runs from reality'
'Hey! You! Why have you climbed up there?
What's that you're suggesting?
What are you up to with that zeppelin milk?'
'A doctor'd be very welcome
if he'd plaster up your imagination!'
'To hell with you.'
'Boo!'
'Have you got a licence?'
In the end I was forced to descend
I'd grown bored of being young . . .
At the hospital as through a window five doctors
stared at my death.
One tapped my chest.
I told him to enter despite the fact that for some time
I'd not even been living there.
'All the better,' he answered, 'we'll hire you out.'
And here I am now at your disposal
cheap,
comfortable,
and keen for you to play dice for my orange shirt.

IN TERROR OF GOOD NATURE

As I'm inclined to observe everything
from the worst possible angle
I'm beginning to believe that the gods, pushed by a tide of beer,
actually reach our table where we naturally gossip
about their possible impossible existence
until smiling they disappear into Hades on luxury bicycles.
Edible reality: I go down to the beach
and instead of water find a sign
saying SEA FORBIDDEN
and because the wild swarm of wasps
chases a car on the highway
and because the ones who've been tied to the stake
now carry that wood
all that's left for me is to ask
how's your family
how's your cancer doing
how are you treating your freedom,
man of the street,
half a brick eaten away by the temple,
the other half in a derelict home
you who believe in the milk bottle left on the step
clerk, railwayman, match-seller,
prophet of time-tables,
you get angry at the meter man
and don't believe that a whale can create its ocean
in public squares
and you won't know whether to call police or ambulance
when menacingly from my throat
springs a jet of happiness, or blood

DYNAMITE

I am the reliable youngster
you usually see on buses
loaf under arm like a camera.
Developing its centre: the flock of sparrows would be wiped out
by the contagious disease of indifference
from the skin of fruit we would extract divine petrol
from sentiments – rubber for boots
(only the beauty of women is too volatile a fuel).
As a reward at night I hear the cooing
of water pipe pigeons
electricity throwing its underskirts
over the civilization of talking ants.
Conceited sadness – this is your account:
there'll come a time when I think myself dynamite
and get out of the town
to explode in joy

LENS

Oh, it's death who from the mirror my image sends
in turn gold, a child, ash.
I'm nothing but a dusty lens
through which time gazes with a laugh.

THE BULLDOZER

What's the use of friends
when one morning, bored, you turn on the cooker
to heat up your tea
and match in hand
hesitating
you suddenly dice with death?
They always respond to cancer with a bunch of grapes
for a time they're ready to say nice things of you
sometimes even smash a glass to your memory
donate you a pint of blood
which'll enrage your cheeks at the first booze up
they trace your image in a field of sugar beet
until cancer is proved not to be cancer
and wonder changes to disappointment
and your recovery begins to seem dubious and in bad taste
and from now on the one thing that'll move you
I mean really move you
won't be the ticking of the clock
or music
or freedom
just the bulldozer –
moving your chair

CHINESE NICKNACKS

In the year two hundred B.C.
the (Chinese) poet Li-Ber
peeling an orange
discovered a small ballerina inside
who'd been lost in a forest
during the No-Tank dynasty.
In the year 1986
I, while excitedly peeling an orange
was suddenly overcome by a wave of mercuric sulphate
and the little worm
now ruler of that core
shouted at me furiously:
'Stop believing in legends, fool.'

PARALLEL LIVES

Without pain I count the stars
just like the crab
who counts the white cells of the drowned.

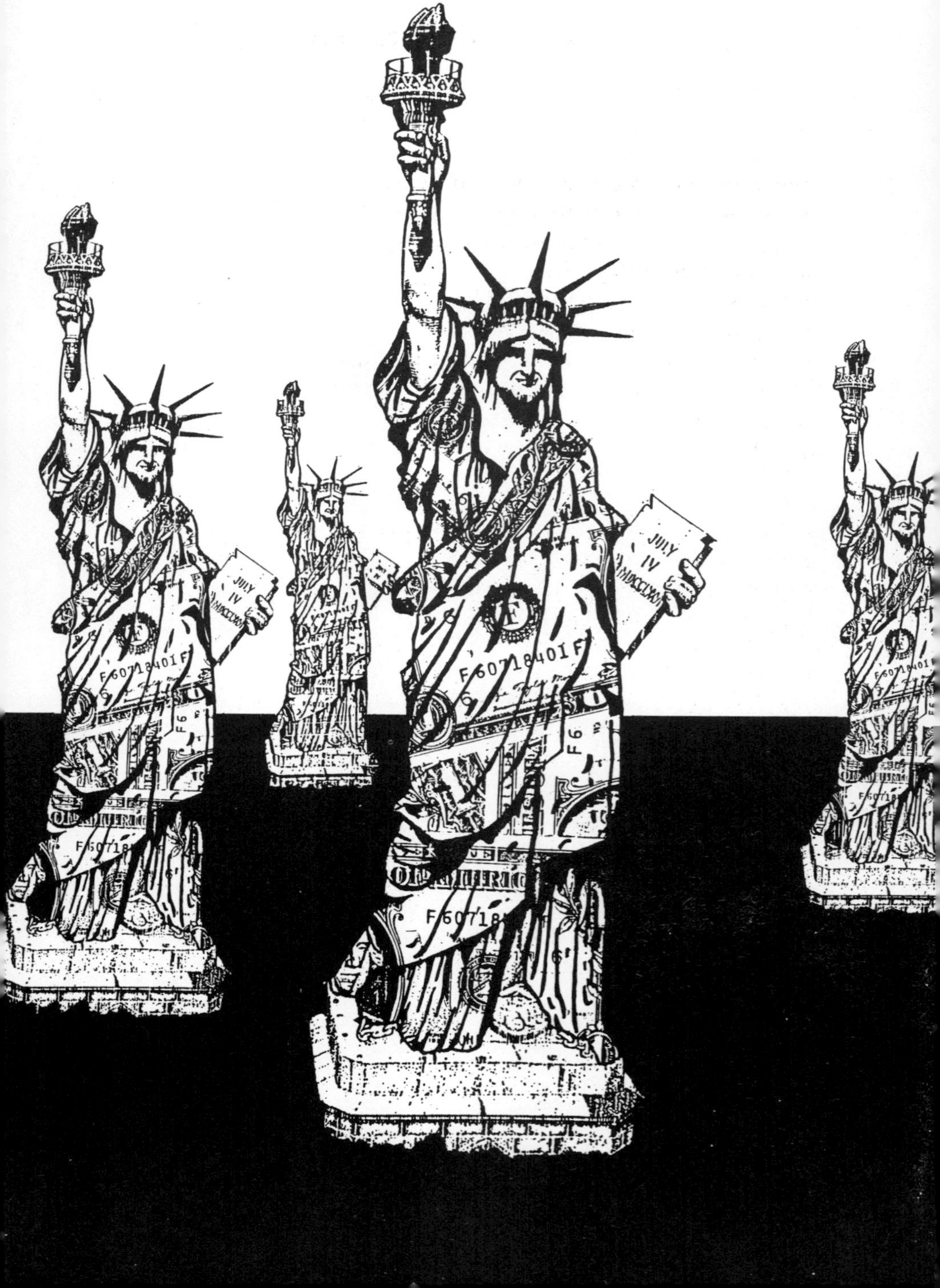
JULY
IV
F 60718401 F

SNAILS' CHANCES

In half a water melon
thrown onto the shore
seventeen snails booze wheels upwards
not wanting to know that off shore
sailors now throw sheaths not messages
and the ones with yachts
those with oysters in their bellies
skinflints - owners of sky scrapers
the ones from the big companies
and even wigmakers, stokers, aloof waiters
Lily, Mary, Greta
girls who can make a dozen cute pants
just from a reel of cotton
the ones stuck like chewing gum
to benches in third class compartments
professional mutineers
experienced hunters – those who seize
the franc, the lei, the pound
all of them layered in the froth of the cocktail
from the well known recipe of Marx
they ask for a souvenir fragment from the Statue of Liberty
to display in the sitting-room on top of the telly
show to envious neighbours
give to the invalid uncle
give to the child to play with
and in the end drop it down the lavatory
willy nilly
they'll break the greenish peel and die
frightened by their own liberty
which for so long they've mixed up with the sugar

THE COMPUTER

Those who faced with wars gargle with camomile,
run with a ladle to catch butterflies
break tiny morcels of martyrs' haloes
enter church with the organ in their belly
pick their noses while others dig their own graves
flush the lavatory so their crying's not heard
search in the rubbish for a new religion
dream of flashy cars but end with a bag of chips
through an operation get rid of their obsession with angels
ignore the beauty of violence,
the idealist, the shy, the musical ones,
shoe-shiners of words
don't see how the town rises into the air
peeing into the sea
how the Himalayas descend from the boat
with suitcases full of paratroopers
how the iron heated by excitement
crunches a mouse
how neurotic forests approach sanatoriums
at the time of trading in people's happiness
while action eats up the song
while we die cheering.

TRANSFIGURATION

The rose has lost its smell
yet it's able to mince a pound of flesh
just as well
shoved under the tongue of the ocean
it'll swim with the oil slick in its teeth
and just as in the latest anatomy books
the heart is drawn like a tumour
at the hour of the contagious sunset, please
stop kissing me – my blood gushes out
cut my veins quickly – so I can breathe

JOB IN LOVE

You make me uglier with your sadness
and understanding turns to fright
and the smile turns off the little light
on the lips forgotten by some kiss

and between barking and budding
April is a place for drinking
the dumb go down with talking
and we're just two planks bedding

Oh if only I could catch a cloud
live in a river sleep in a mallow
to be a sort of walking hollow
where an actor grows old

to give performances for little or less
ridiculous as a king among doves
to carry your loneliness to a wilderness
a happy Job in a castle of boils

MENAGERIE

The animal in me
listens to the monotonous brooding of days
and feels like singing
cheerfully postponing death on the streets
raises eyes to the sky as if to a toy stall
while the brother of the cuckoo
looks at the clock in the tower
as if something were to be taken from the table
he pushes the blanket to one side
as if opening a hospital door
until the swarm of churches is heard
buzzing above that wretched crucified one
and I begin to understand – I'm the only one who doesn't cover
                                                                                                his face
at the sight of curved lightning over the manger
of oxen implanted in the rose–pink sky

LETTER TO MY MOTHER

You tell me that rats have gnawed the church to its roots
my sad mother
and yet our faith has more to do with
bread and wine,
as long as oats aren't laid
in my sister's bed, she who ran away to the fields
as long as the singer driven into nature
doesn't go to the wild,
over death which combs you
over entrails of the fire
storks pass like leukemia of stars

IN ALL INNOCENCE

Green belly button of death tying up angelical loonies
when the hour strips us of our destiny
Mary sells her child in churches
forever deceived by the male Deity.

The apple's always looking for the worm
and the wise man's gag is love-in-a mist,
angel feathers fill pillows in turn
and the cross in all innocence invites another guest

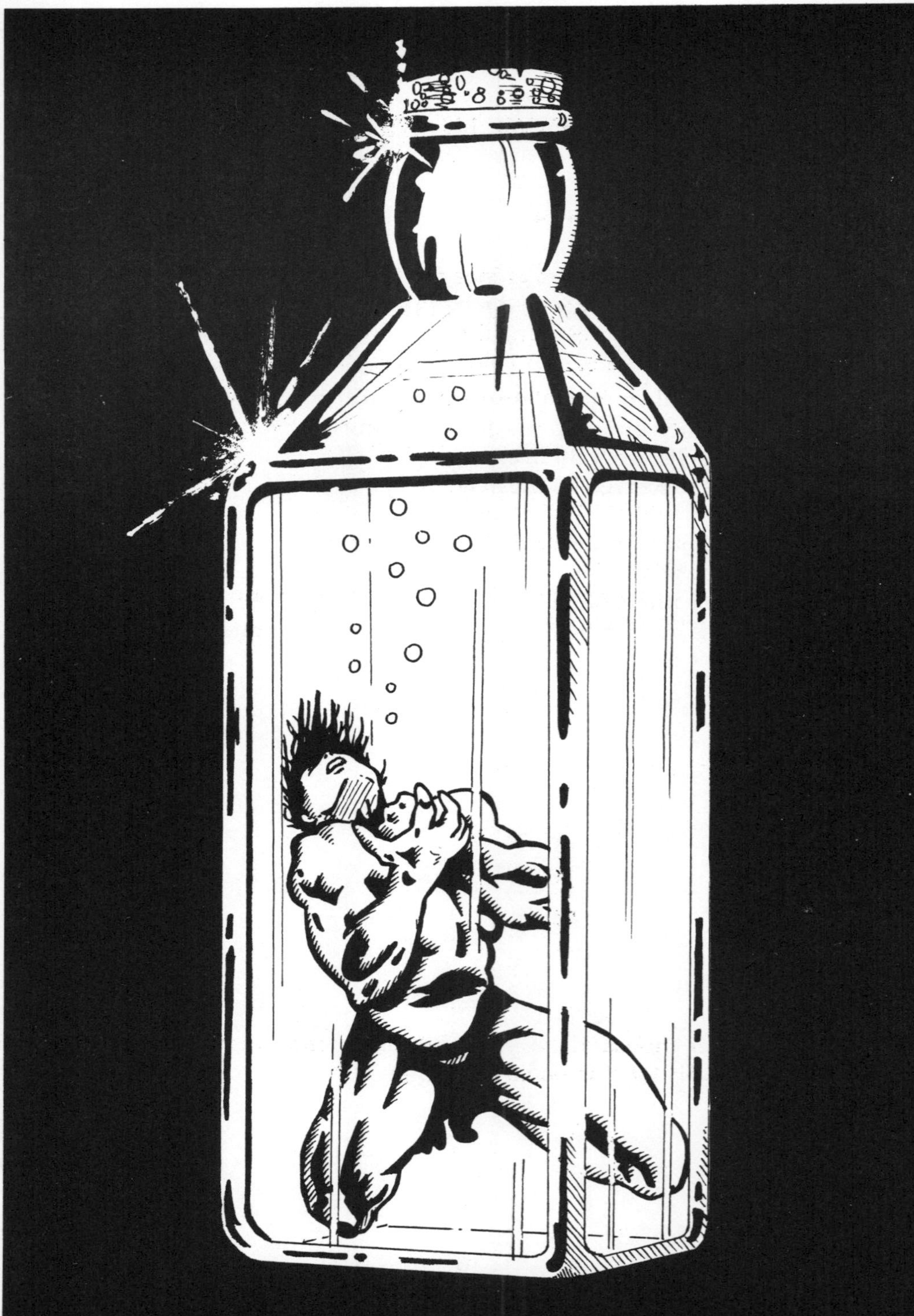

NEWS IN BRIEF

When from car exhausts
skylarks soar
you won't anymore be a guinea pig of modern civilization.
In return you'll have seen the baby sleeping on newspaper
and thanks to the pestering flies
naked skin showing lead-coloured letters
imprinted on his pink bum
news in brief
definitely browsed by the well-meaning rain:

one   anyone spitting on mirrors hasn't got a mum
two   somewhere they play skittles with the bodies of unknown soldiers
three   twice a week the prodigal sun visits the old folks' home in a golden car
four   goats continue to be goats
five   the hair of the young curls on the wheels of industry
six   the rat has passed like Spring through girls' boarding schools
seven   the angel sells posters from his period of enforced silence

eight   space left for your soul..

        ....

        ....

        ....

nine   for thousands of years I'll retreat into a jar of alcohol to wait for this poem to appear.

REFECTORY

Some wretched people
are thrown by chance between the slices of bread
of a sandwich at the table of the gods.
With shoulders full of crumbs
hunchbacked by so much glory
modern penitenciaries sweat under their tongues.
They're not hit in the spring by the wave of beautiful women
dragging them to God knows what pub,
their stomachs held in by pins
and too early do they carry a church between their legs.
Of course they allow whistling in the bathroom
the mechnical ecstasy
and absurd sacrifice,
inventors of a more dangerous moral than the neutron bomb,
they die on a Sunday
so that on Monday their faces will substitute
the greasy globs in soup
and make us happy once again
here in Kamchatka
at this refectory near the Equator
where I dip my feet into the Black Sea.

A COUPLE

This evening the car gets into my clothes
whimpers like a child until windows become misty
a wave of heat changes people
into happy cake crumbs
flowers flash like a field's sparking plugs
kisses start turbines moving
butterflies pass under the earth towards gardens of ore
that's where I wait for you my love to watch the sea
I won't caress your hair crammed in comfortable mattresses
but we'll make love silently under cold boilers
until the boat reaches its destination
and the mechanic taps my knees
and another cleans me of the smoke of illusion
ready for the new journey
you'll give me
your petrol breath my love

HIRED SUN

I am an oil stain on the tall windows,
on your life, starched daily,
neither force nor rain will make me disappear
just as the small change in the beggar's pocket
attracts lightning
in silver cutlery
I'll conceal
the rat killed by watchmen in the garden
on the peel of the melon you'll find
a poem purposely etched with my nail
and there it is a crack in the wall
through which one of your girls will run off with the poor student
but you withdraw to the cheap hired sun
celebrating your indigestion
let it bark, you'll say,
let it bark,
you don't even throw it a bone anymore
but stretch out calmly under rays of my shining fangs

THE CONTEMPORARY GOAT

The goat eats roses of municipal gardens
munches trams like raw peas
never goes to the office in the morning
never reads the evening paper
strips telegraph poles like mulberry trees
unashamedly ignores all traffic lights
doesn't want a luxury car and I swear
hasn't yet patented plastic grass
although it does know a little about forests;
the town sways in swings of smoke
they've replaced the statue in the centre now
only this stubborn goat
gives milk and never once asks how

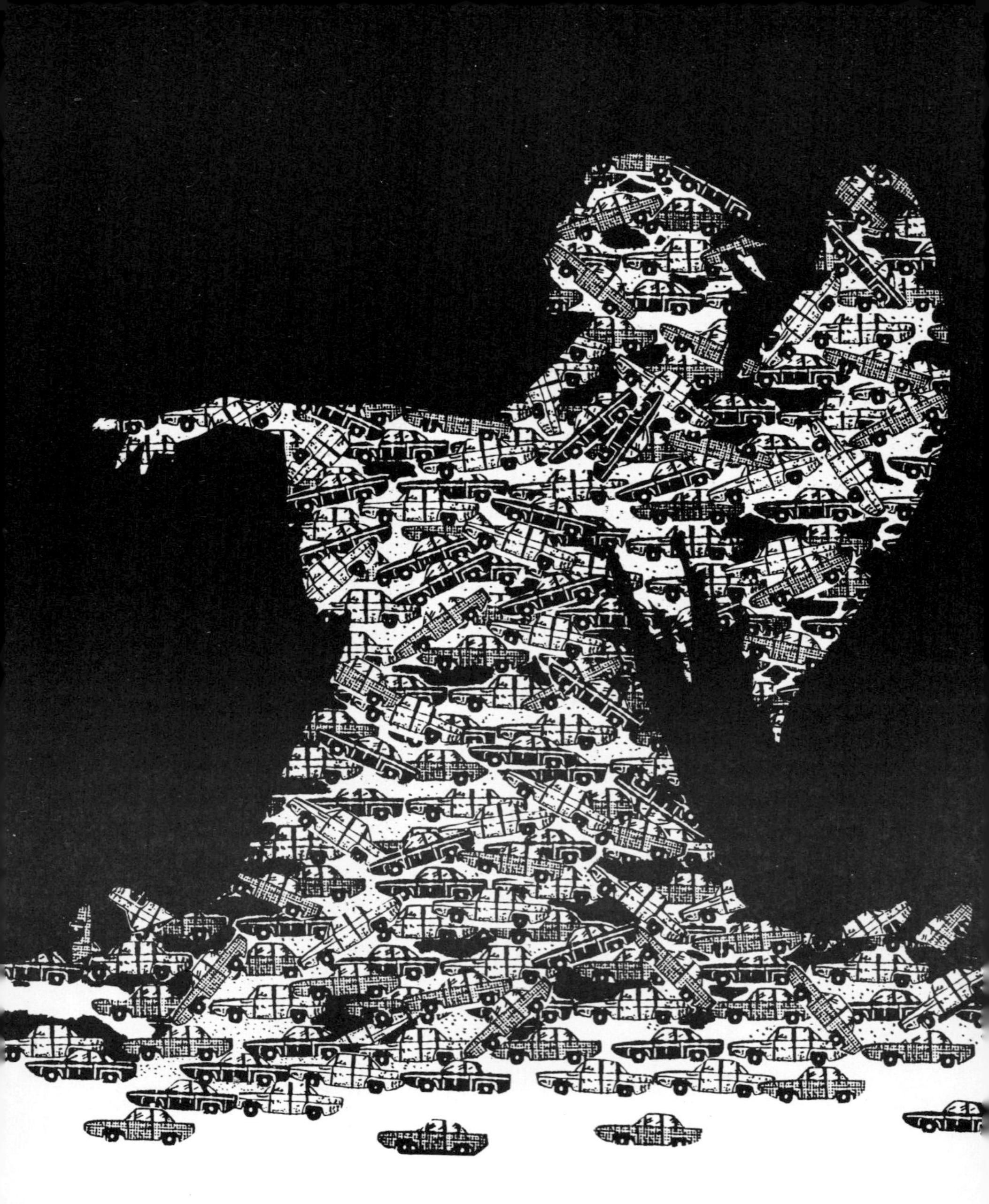

RUSTING

Because we've already put governments on the moon
we'll soon invent bread with teeth
a mechanical rainbow to cut the rain
an icon to appear before us on caterpillar tracks . . .

As at a fair you pull out graves from a sleeve
dear Lord,
by the light of Your dim halo
glory will polish its own boots
the monkey will swing between the hands of the clock.
Why haven't You got the sweet recklessness of the madman
to pull towns with a string towards the woods?
Polluted seas will beat their waves
migrating towards pure stars

In the cars' cemetery I saw an angel rusting.

IT'S NOT SNOWING

As if I were trading in falling stars
poetry is still profitable
bringing me immense earnings of advice, summonses,
whistling whips through public telephones.

Oh defiant diffidence of the beggar
always ready to invent a tiny church
for casual worshippers.

Of course I have the right
I have the right to imagine
you mirroring yourself with your golden hair
sizzling in the skin of a buffalo
while I
in the polished boots of art
refuse to comb mine.

Don't rejoice
it's not snowing
above us they're spitting, bored by paradise

ABSURD CHESS

Sweet innocence
to believe that poetry can improve the world.
It's as if throwing a lump of sugar
into a tiger's cage
would start it reading Shakespeare.
Fattened by your own misfortunes
(as if you'd lunched in a mirror)
you whistle like a train in a station
until the crowd squashes you underfoot
in a hurry to take up that warm, cosy place on your neck
and because dream is but a bastard of reality,
remember the absurd game of chess
where the mad knight moved villages
first sacrificing the horses,
and a thousand people hurried out to praise his game

EVOLUTION OF DREAM

Festivities of winter are coming – where can we mirror ourselves
when spitoons have crammed their chrome under wrapping paper?
Just as the ostrich
no longer wants to know
I'm ready to go on being duped
but I just have the feeling it won't be long before snow's
                                          rationed with coupons
I'm ready to go on accepting the ornate boredom
but the magi parachuted into town
as if foretelling the birth of a smarmy film star
are peddling luxury soaps
cigarettes smelling of paradise and doom.
And look, while waiting for the glory of Nothingness to turn
our cowardness has frozen it forever:
the road sweeper dreams he's a roadsweeper
the honourable one dreams himself honourable
and the worm, that he's a worm.

MONOLOGUE WITH A MOUSE

To reach the castle
I climb into an oily car
as if primed by bellows of an accordion
pumped by the merriness of gypsies.
In their looks
the outskirts of civilization decant their spirited contempt:
the knife doesn't ask what you're called,
the sour wine and smell of dung on the boots
give the oaths a note of familiar greeting.
Their poverty isn't terrifying
(proof is the stork's low flight when looking for a nest)
they have no church as they already know all about each other
fascinated like wild rabbits
in the blinding light of crime
they have time to throw over the town
a handful of jangling children.
I live in a sort of kitchen in a real castle
I'm a ridiculous bloke:
I carry images in a wheelbarrow
I catch a mouse in my cap because I want to talk to it
and it dies of heart failure
unable to put up with my love, boredom,
loneliness or song

from
Nature's Democracy
Democraţia naturii
(1981)

NATURE'S DEMOCRACY

In March rubbish bins explode splashing
the neorealist darkness
with cats red as flames.
The town simmers beneath their lustful phosphorous
the kiss smelling sweetly of sulphur.
Pregnant women would suddenly float through the room
if it weren't for those heavy sacks of sand
carping before the telly
blowing into eternal soups.
Hosts of butterflies pass under girls' skirts
and my hand falls heavy with pollen.
If they installed a small power station now
at the mouth of fools
it'd surely work full blast
(indolent and poor I'm not even afraid anymore).
A child pees on the church tower
and God receives his warm jet
as if comfort to an aching heel.
The rotten potato thrown on waste ground
pokes out HIS little willy
as a sign of nature's democracy

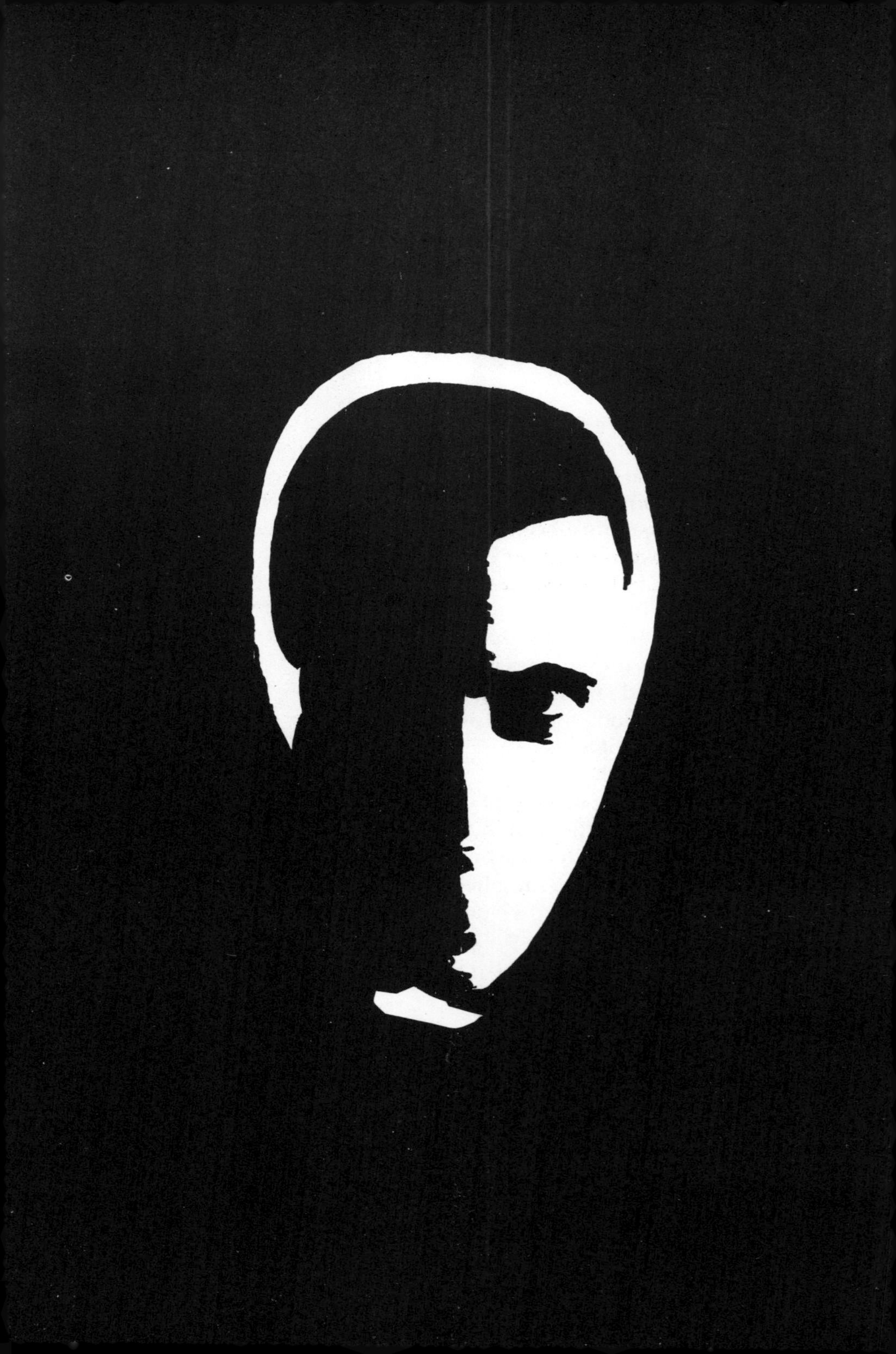

PEST CONTROL

Somebody comes
with a deadly smelling cannister on his back:
'Who are they, those weak, wretched people
hidden behind the furniture?'
My parents who survived the first world war
and the second
but this time they'll find it hard

MANUSCRIPT FOUND IN A BOTTLE LAMP

A cold pair of scissors for cutting fingers
has nested in the letter box.

On the cathedral hill there are shop windows but no shops.

In the station a dwarf walks his Philips hump
waiting for clients.

Death's freely available and cheap enough
while in contrast
there's great saving on fuel, paper and God.

If idiots were edible
there'd be a smaller queue at the butchers for intellectuals

SOME ADVICE FOR THE HONEYMOON

Get ready to love me
which means put on the white coat
buy me a wheelchair
take the laurel wreath from off my head
and with its leaves make me herbal tea instead

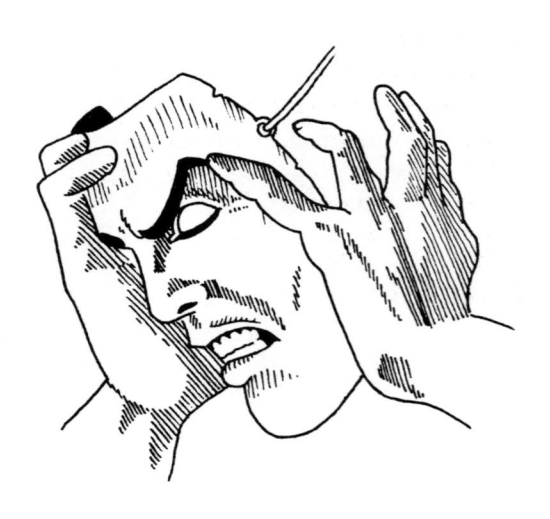

TRAVELLING PLAYERS

Oh God how I was born
red with anger
crying out in an unknown tongue
charged with lightning and airs of a great actor
and how I'll die
cowering and just carrying a tray
overcome by stage fright before death
like an amateur on provincial boards
with the promptor suffocated in the wings of the chest

SEVEN DRAWERS

ONE
In the evening she combs her hair
and a cloud of electric bees swarm through it:
a silken chair
where a happy man
will be sentenced to death by electrocution.

TWO
A boat sinks groaning
under the weight of tired butterflies
landed on the masts

THREE
You've only got to tickle the pyramid a bit
for the mummy to burst out laughing
from under the nappies.

FOUR
On Saturday night
the sea undoes its zip shamelessly.

FIVE
The oil gurgling freely on the Steppes,
now lights the lamp in front of which
you're made to speak,
tables turned about.

SIX
A hydro-electric dam blown up
by roe of hysterical fish.

SEVEN
Why haven't I got a light canoe
amongst herons and reeds and natives
at the mouth of a river to carry seeds and myrrh
to call uah uah with hand to my mouth
in the old Indian dialect
to hear the answer uah uah
from the loudspeakers on the shore

SKIMPY BIOGRAPHY

Some can't wait to see me floating
like Ophelia, newspaper tiara on head,
but tired by so much invention
they enter my biography gravely as into a leper colony
ready to mark the white zones and shout:
danger of contamination
musical virus
tear-carrying bacteria
dog with delayed effects
eyes bulging at the golden hams of the West says he's not too
                                                                                                  hungry
keeps on singing stupidly like the juke-box refusing money
his father in the engine shed smells lavender secretly
his mother carries boxes growing gradually deaf
                          (we assume she doesn't want to hear)
his sister a teacher of the mentally handicapped feels
                                                                            free free free
about his brother nothing's known which is even worse
the existence of this family makes him tolerant
but he has an odd way of loving his country which is
                                                                             very worrying
and in no way can we extract the sweet earth from his mouth
without the churches of his native land crumbling

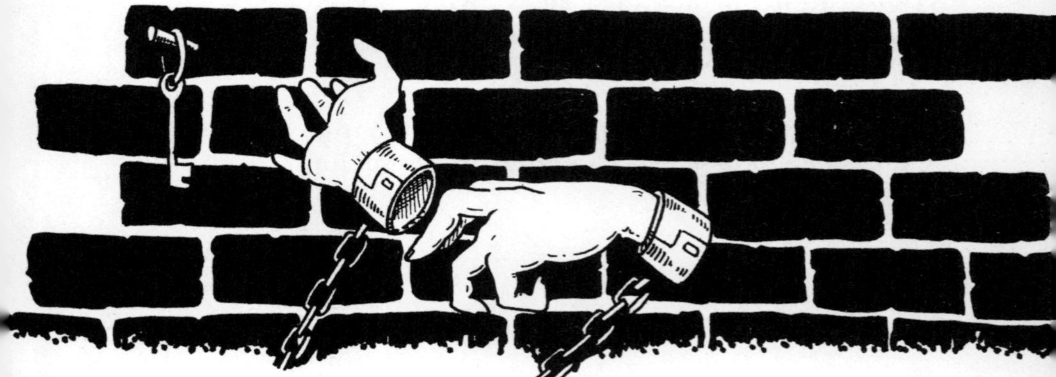

WALLS

Stupid illusion:
to surround oneself with walls
then suddenly to feel
so free

COLD COMFORT

God preserve me from those who want what's best for me
from the nice guys
always cheerfully ready to inform on me
from the priest with a tape recorder under his vestment
from the blanket you can't get under without saying good evening
from the dictators caught in the chords of the harp
from those angry with their own people
now when winter's coming
we have neither tall walls
nor geese on the Capitoline
only great provisions of tolerance and fear

COWS

These cows brought by air from Holland
are the pride of our district
I swear
seven gypsies hired to play to them softly
stay hidden in the maize until evening
offended, the cowherds hiccup under showers
sneeze under X-ray machines
and the doctor scolds them
for the reek of tobacco and booze on their clothes.
If it hadn't been for the blind villages around
and the barefooted children in the grazing
somewhat spoiling the landscape
those ballerinas would have won even more medals

SONG

In the morning you die cheap rate
at lunchtime, regarded well,
but the evening's a must for acclaim
the sun seems like a rake
the lake a sickle
with which I'm cutting my diamond vein.

A cap's a cloth shell
where I can lose my mind
like God in a balloon
–death with gossip and alcohol
in the middle of a crowd
a dog accordion.

However it's warm as inside a mammal
and the houses store
a strange vibration
my ramshackle angel
or
old fashioned heaven

AVALANCHE

On the 11th of November at nine in the morning
I'd made a date
with a young avalanche of snow
in the Himalayas
on the sweetest slope in the world.
What love at first sight it could have been,
but by the time my passport was ready
my next of kin declared
my luggage packed
my ticket bought
the customs man had searched me
the detectors sniffed me,
at a quarter past nine
offended and hysterical
it ran off further down with a Greek and two Japanese . . .

Oh God, sweeten such institutions of sadness
those institutions which fight against love
against love and death

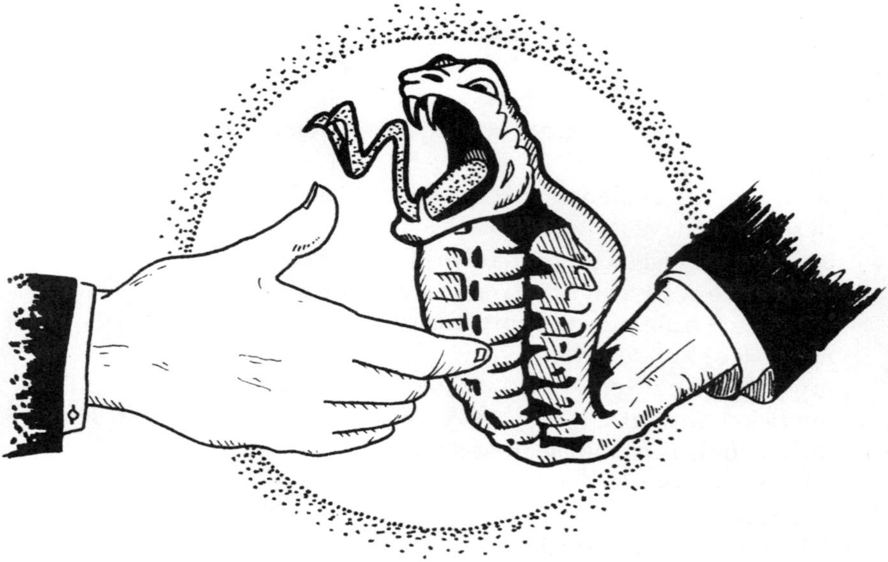

LOVE STORY

A former friend
who proved to be a talented informer
having produced three children with the help of a woman
and having married her off to a dentist who was emigrating
                                                to America
(a splendid deal, good-bye, good-bye!)
dug himself even deeper into his native land
and produced honey with the help of some bees
about which he complained to the Police
because they were feeding on pollen from plants facing the
                                                    West,
then he produced a few friends
much easier to manoeuvre than hives
non-stop production winter and summer
occasionally slithering a yellow viper
into your sleeve
when shaking hands,
very convincingly
when detecting – a baby cancer in the pallor of your cheek
     – truth in the rumour that your love is unfaithful
when selling you – a lamp which in fact was Lenin's
     – a wardrobe without doors so any woman could leave you.
In the end I told him: please be so good
as to make yourself my real enemy. . .
and my God how well he succeeded

THE SIGN SEARCHER

At the end of the line
serene gypsies sell poisonous mushrooms
the bootblack reads the life of Napoleon
the artist is none other than the client of the shaky barber,
only the brandy factory rises clearly above the rest
its aluminium humbles the church
plastic barrels shine like icons
water dresses up as wine,
God as a pipeline,
the magi guided by X-rays
knock in your chest as at a sanatorium door,
pretend you don't hear
because spring is coming
otherwise why are even foxes stained with oil,
those clerks sneaking away to the woods;
further down certainly
at the mouth of the Danube
tac tac a sewing machine scrapes together coots and pelicans
or shooting is heard
pretend you don't hear because spring is coming
and the humming of the town dries your tears:
the small explosion of laddered tights on girls' thighs
wolf whistling of young soldiers in the tiny station
the squeaking of the hungry mouse in the letter box
and the laughing of those in lorries on top of cheap furniture

ONE FACTORY CALLS FOR ANOTHER

Every month a hundred women run away
from the hostel at the silk factory
looms bark in vain
the production graph crawls to the floor
the manager turns grey
the phone swears
dollars green with anger tiptoe back to the West,
slogans are written larger and larger
meetings get fiercer
lorries bring girls from nearby villages
to train 'on the job'
but every month a hundred women run away
excited like bulls at the sight of red silk
in a ring without toreadors or blood.
If only they'd hurry with the bulldozers
to level the ground
labourers and steel workers
drivers who know how to wolf whistle
ageing yobbos, building site artists,
to make conveyor belts rumble
and Siemens Martins' furnaces sing
to bring the smell of coal and pitch
to settle the girls down
hand in hand
silk and smelt
factory next to factory

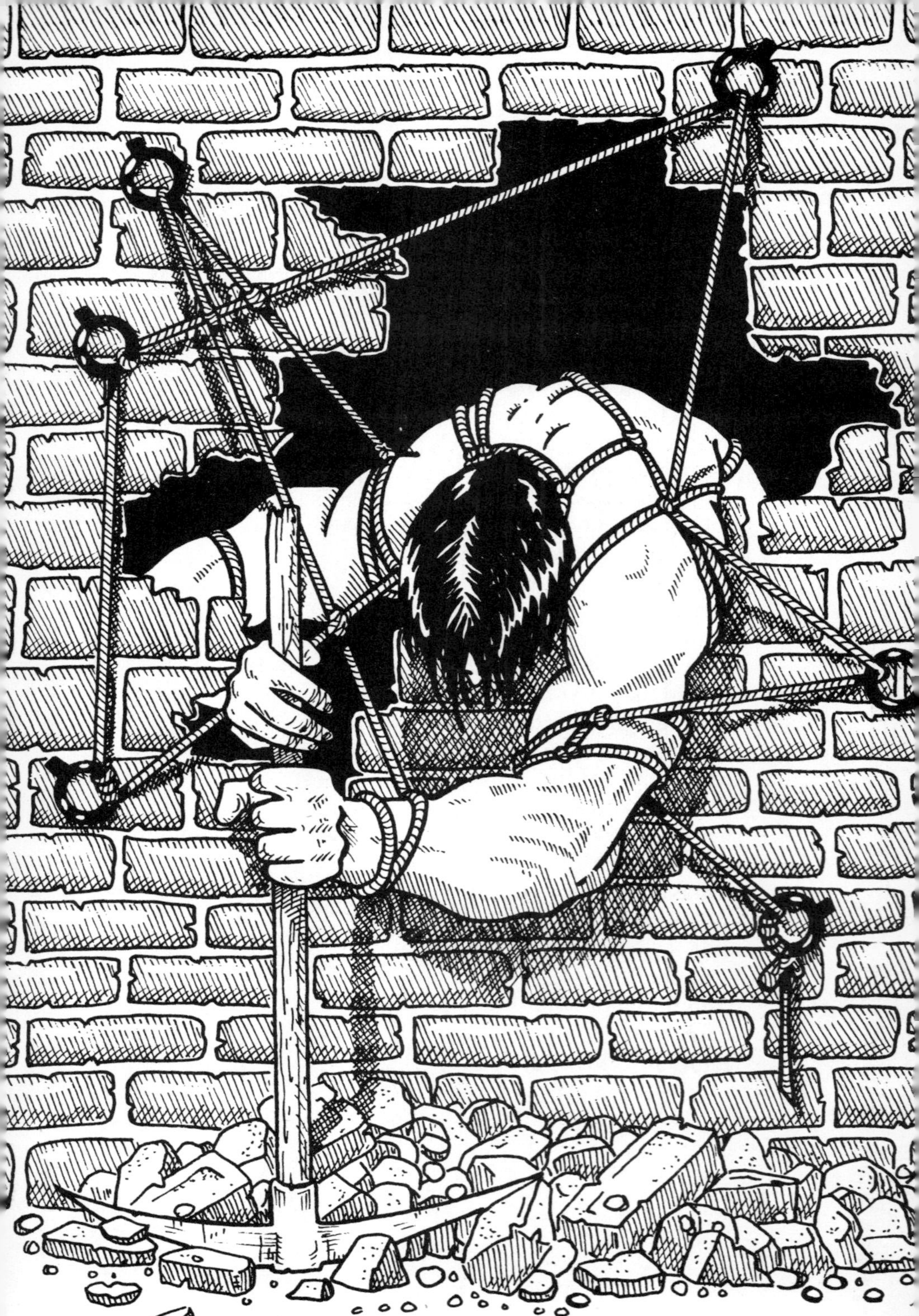

DISCOVERING . . .

For a long time I thought poetry slept beneath a heron's wing
or that I'd have to forage for it in forests
but like a prophet driven from the wilderness by gurgling oil
I'm now ready to make a pact with reality
and admit to having been wrong:
I'm smashing the wall with a pickaxe
so you can see

THE SHORT-SIGHTED PAINTER

Many madmen have thought themselves generals
and some have even become them,
the short-sighted decorator of eggs will one day decorate a church
and a comet might even collide with its dome
calling to it: 'Christ has risen'
and so with you,
you who swear you love me,
perhaps, one day in the future, will

SPEECH AGAINST REVOLT

Unproductive and hysterical
revolt hasn't brought ME large stretches of land
at night it slips under the blanket with me
by day, electrocutes me on the field
give me a melon on which I can rest
give me a moving train on which I can lean
because unashamedly I get hungry at the stake
and instead of a spine I have a loaded cartridge case
growl growl I pretend to be both dog and hunter
and even the native hounded in the swamps,
I no longer love myself, so I'll grow old
and God is a bottomless pocket
and loneliness is forever creating
the same amateurs of self slaughter
I want to be born but my mother says she's had enough.
I want to weep but others show more talent,
give me a melon to rest on
give me a moving train to lean on

VILLAGE WITH COMMUTERS

I do the best I can and bring prosperity to friends
with my red shirt reeking of fried fish
I slip into church with a case of beer to keep it cold
while the priest plays backgammon with the militia
and well-heeled gypsies carve a new groove on the stereo
because today is Monday Tuesday Wednesday Thursday
                                                        Friday Saturday
and the dog's skin will be used for bellows of an accordion
and the fire extinguisher for a small illegal still.
Towards evening
a train whistles at the edge of the village
and leaves in the air a stink of lavender and commuters
lads swearing and laughing
faces I've never seen before
and I don't know what the hell they're doing here

A SHORT EXTRACT FROM THE SECRET FILES OF THE 100 YEARS WAR

The importance of the little mouse in the 100 years war
is easily denied by deaf chroniclers of the time
or even (and unjustly so) entirely overlooked:
'All you had to do was roll across the floor
for the princess to throw herself fluttering
into the arms of the stable boy
the maid under the robe of the indulgent priest
the cook into the basket of cucumbers, wink, wink . . .
Your squeak has brought into the world
a few dozen nobles with fresh blood
merchants and geniuses
inventors and countless rogues,
you poor pretext of nature
symbol of natural instinct
tool of democracy on earth'

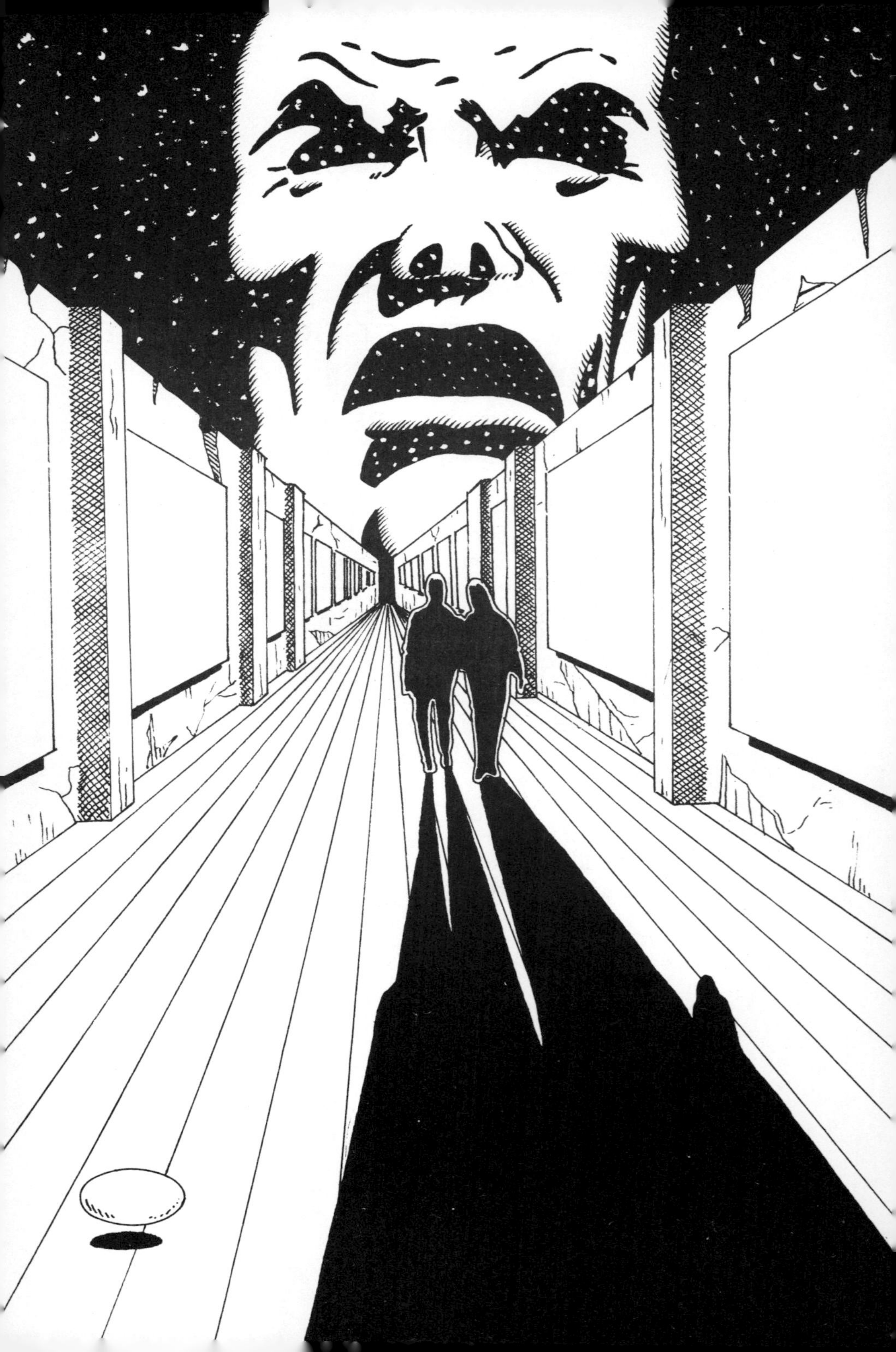

HENS

In a castle turned into a battery farm
boozing till dawn
with the caretaker and the watchman
we drank beetroot wine – and we didn't care
white wine from rotten wood – and we didn't care
the hens hadn't much political awareness
they clucked under their breath and turned a blind eye
pecked at the paint on pictures
scratched in Breughel the Elder
clucked in the clavichord
laid eggs in the Biedermeier
(from their wattles Savonarola could have made himself a
                                                     first rate cassock)
we were happy
and ready to go lion hunting
with fly paper,
the revolution was smelling of baked potatoes
loud speakers had replaced all art
there were also lamps giving out darkness
also letter boxes left unopened
and we also clucked under our breath
we also turned a blind eye

TITANIC WALTZ

Pedlar of my own death
smuggler with suitcases full of coughing
my bones resound in me: jingle jangle
and the little monks of gastric juices emerge begging
at large airports
in basements
at stations
a sort of cultural ambassador
with holes in my pockets
a squashed wasp buzzing poems
a sunken ship leaving behind
not even a waltz
in front of the sandwich vending machine
I pray
to the rattling coins
for my little provincial town to fall
between two slices of bread
jingle jangle
behind the currency exchange
in a glaring lavatory
I deposit the gold ingots of my bladder
(Heh! Redundant God of poor poets
where the hell are you?)
since birth I've been followed by a fleecy lined iceberg
a transistorised God first swallowing up my name
staring at me with all its floors
then suddenly crushing me with all its cogs
on a big wave of newspapers
under the big wave of newspapers
jingle jangle

THE FUGITIVE

Keep for yourself that nice sugar lump
lead yourself up the garden path, be your own trainer
for autumn's beginning to look just like a camp
and you like a fugitive spied on from the tower,

there's striped melons everywhere and from lamps acid's
                                                                                      raining
potatoes in trenches, rivers in uniform
as if from nature Switzerland were gently disappearing
nothing's neutral so everything sides with them.

Then you're ready to make a castle from a cotton weave
sell your cry too cheaply and bow down low at doors
absent-mindedly like a bee that mistakes a lamp for a hive
and turns all its pollen into ashes

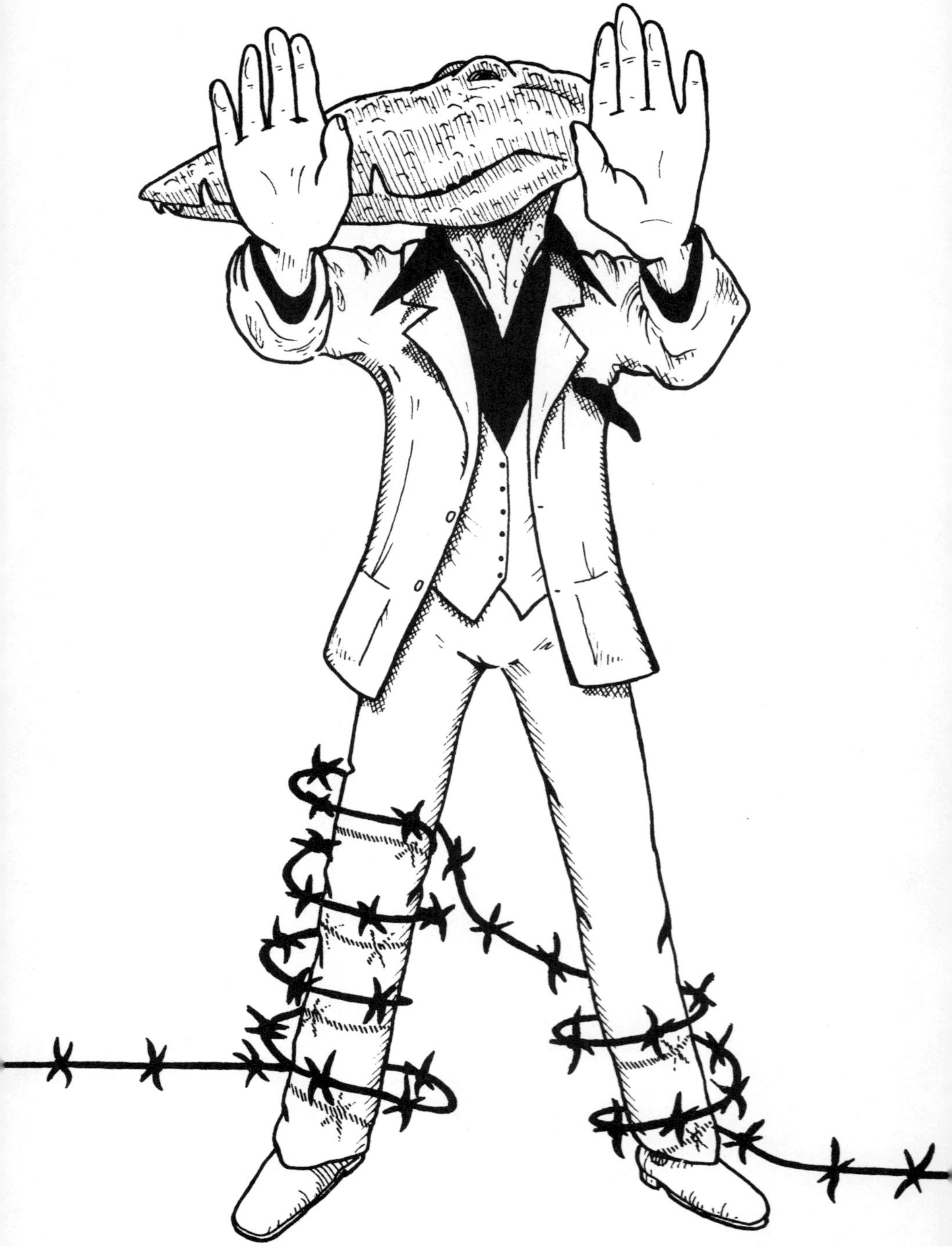

HOW THE NATIVES ON THE RESERVATION LOST THE RIGHT TO TRAVEL

A crocodile fed up to the back teeth
with the flesh of natives
decided to join in the campaign
for their protection:
with the help of a pusher he sold his skin
bought barbed wire of the highest quality
and surrounded the reservation in such a way
that today
crocodiles can't reach the natives anymore
but neither can the natives travel freely to the States
in the belly of some crocodile

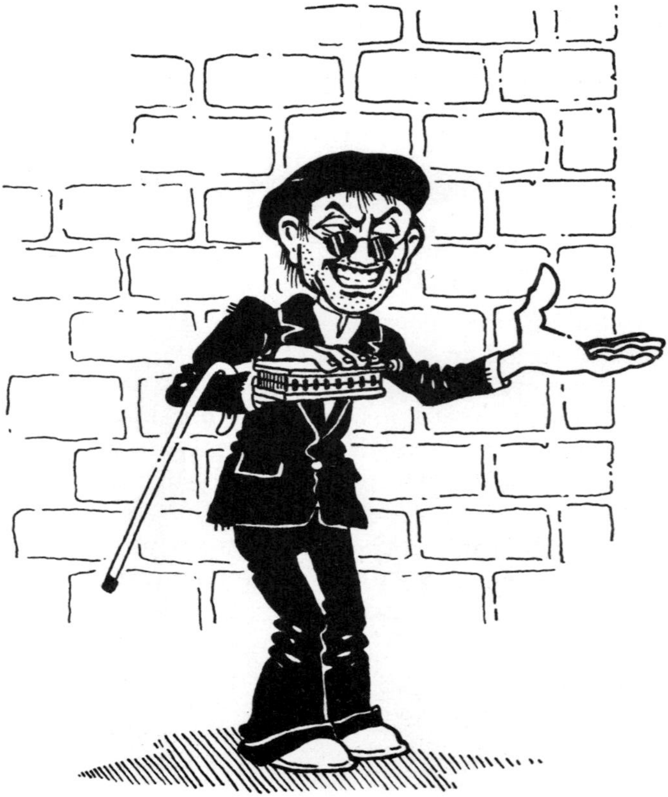

A DAY WITHOUT SANDWICHES

Where two streets clumsily collide with each other
if you're lucky you bump into the blindman with the
                                                   harmonica,
he smiles guiltily
and blows the Blue Danube in your ear,
don't get angry but give him money as fast as you can
if you want to escape with an untorn collar
or pull your chin away from his greasy fingers
so he can't crush you gently with a boot
as if knowing something about your fishy biography
give him the money quickly
be glad you've got away
and give up sandwiches for today

WITH ALL MODESTY

With all modesty
I would retire to the colony of cats in the southern ocean
near the deceptive phosphorus of their eyes
I'd watch ships wrecked
gulp down fish after fish
and miaow for pleasure like an old lecher
after girls of fourteen round apartment blocks,
I wouldn't hear pneumatic drills separating lovers in the
                                                                   hospital,
or the whistle of the gas in the meter
or the hooter at five
fish after fish till the end of my days
licking salt and life from my nails
at night
among small furry ones charged with electricity
attracting disorientated angels
like crumbs of paper in love with ebony

GUERNICA

Where they pass by with their humid imagination
lichen and reindeer bloom
disgusted lamps swallow their own wicks
as wise men swallow their tongues before a tyrant
but gods born in the hum of bars
disappear one night in the southern goods train
condemned without witnesses to a tangled and enforced
                                                                           mythology
to look for the seed of the flute in some marshy reeds God
                                                                 knows where

and to dig their own graves in the rain
so we can find an outlet to the sea . . .
Oh, vulnerable gods, vulnerable gods
death is a homeland without the Press.

HUNGER*

God give us our daily hunger
give us the potato and the onion
the kitchen where frustrations shipwreck
our saliva which reflects the gods.

Happy barbarian
at the edge of an empire
nibbling with his savage hand
the marble grapes
from the cornice of the holy temple.

* In southern India a strange plant grows whose leaves can be chewed allowing man to survive sixteen days without feeling pangs of hunger.

from
Exile on a Peppercorn
Exil pe o boabă de piper
(1983)

WINTER DIARY AT PONTUS EUXINUS (17.A.D.)

It's in a grocer's shop I'd like to disappear
in a coat light as tea leaves,
into my small bit of South at the mouth of the Danube,
among piles of scented boxes . . .
The grocer's kind hearted and tells me
the story of the monkey found in a sack of beans
who died trying to understand the taste of snow.
It's a rather sad story and full of meaning
yet in Rome I know a few
who'd be only too happy to hear it

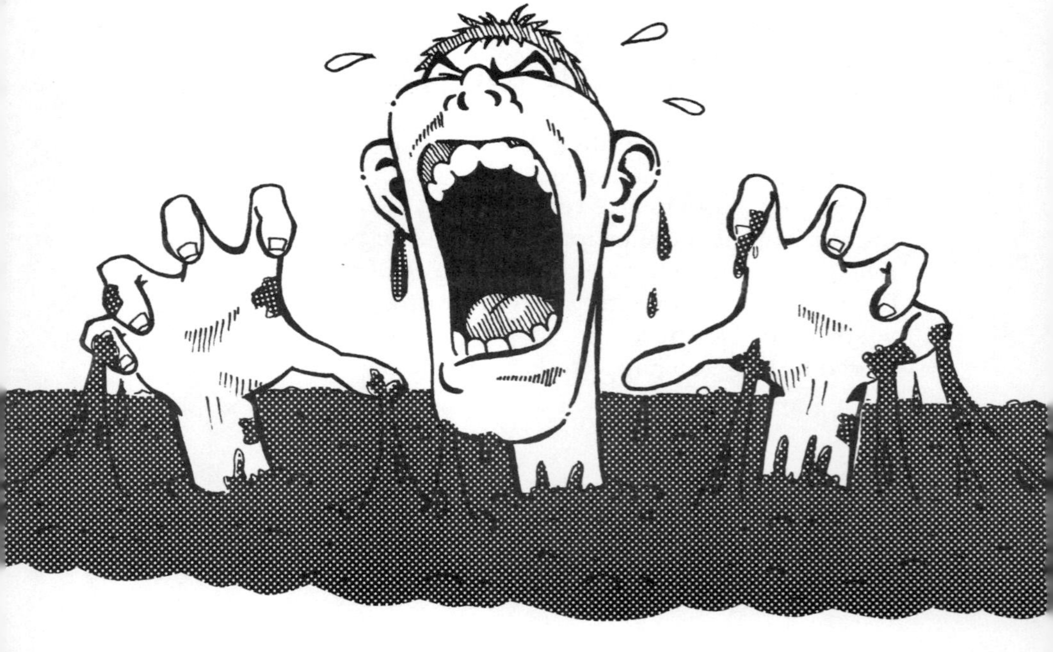

WHO ARE THEY LORD?!

Who are they Lord, these inspectors of nappies
the ones married to forbidden doors
ready to mix up my childhood with a factory
and my blanket with the main line station?!
They turn the key of parable only a little
and the prodigal son returns to the arms of the police
they know how to breathe
to put my light out properly
when the tide deposits madmen on the shore
and the Bedouin inanely
shouts for us to do a belly dance

POSTPONED

The revolt's being postponed because of the rain
the child's being postponed because of the grain
though not only dogs bark at Mary again
though oxen are warm, though the star is aflame
and the magi are in debt to the inn of Pain
and gossip flows beneath the hand's terrain
the child is postponed because of the grain
the revolt's postponed because of the rain

SHIP'S LOG

Ill from the lights in the manger of the Balkans
where the sea ripples even into pub lavatories
with a plank of wood you can make a boat
with a capful of seeds you can be a merchant.
A few grand's all you need
and your papers are in order, to be a Turk or Greek:
Ibrahim, Kazaluki, or Ianis,
only off shore you're clear who you are.
All Europe's in the nearby boat. Come on salute it!
The port's record player licks the froth.
The day slips on the edge of the knife
no longer cutting itself

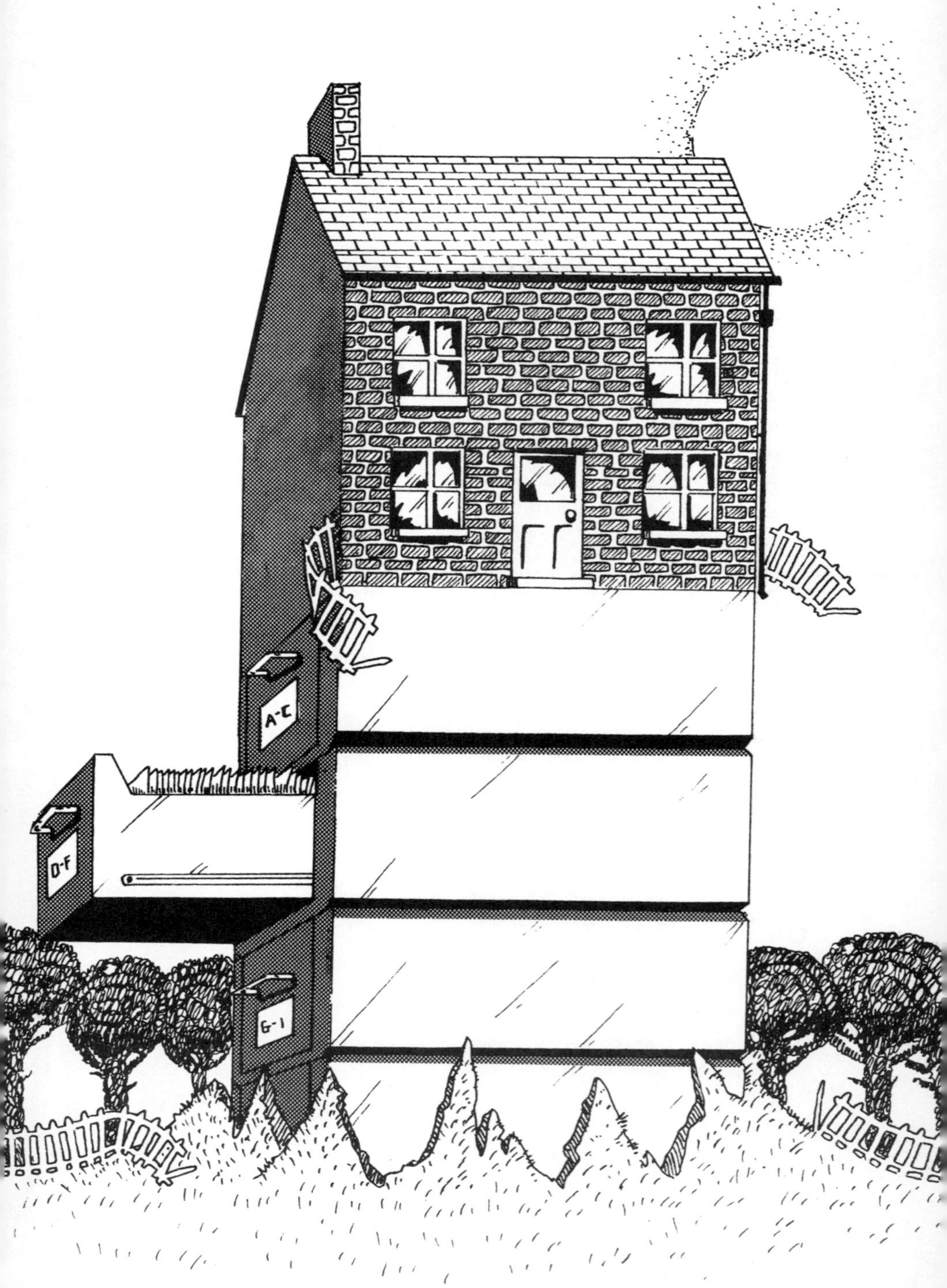

A-C
D-F
G-I

THE ARTIST'S HOME

My dossier grows like a fine loaf
gently leavening it swells, cleaves,
we'll spend a good time together my love
under its vinyl eaves.

So not to be alone we'll take your parents
and just in case take umbrellas please
autumn's in words and only rain in our spoons
and tax inspectors fall from trees.

Today I go carelessly past shop windows
I don't look, or smell or swear:
cannon fodder, cells of bees
and a little vodka angel in the clear azure . . .

SONG

They've opened up some prisons
but no one's come out of them,
some hanged themselves with their dreams
others buried themselves in the walls.

It's no longer possible to create
church or flag from the earth now,
some lift shoulders and with elbows navigate
others bang the threshold with their brow.

Who waits for me can no longer wait
inside me there's no life
the ray falls rancid not straight
a tear's no longer water but a knife.

ONE OF ARMSTRONG'S TUNES

In the evenings when orchestras turn to murder
and on waves of beer seven thousand drunkards leave for
                                      America
knocking for an answer
is the kangeroo from the pregnant virgin's nightmares
pocket chock-a-block with threatening letters.
Go into the street to heal your imagination
as an invalid anything's allowed out of pity or revulsion,
like a cooled volcano
throat stuffed with newspapers and bottles
tonight surprise the tourists
and play on the trumpet of lava
one of Armstrong's tunes

EXILE ON A PEPPERCORN

Let the accountants count the waves
let others shake the keys
be the crow with the violin, the madman, the porter
who in December carries glue to the trees.

All of a sudden feel embarrassed to die,
in marshes with music an athlete of innocence
order girls champagne gladioli
from a portable bed inside the ambulance . . .

And instead of rest choose pepper
so you can salute if it's not too bad
those who put concrete, glass and steel girders
in the space from which God has fled